Internal Organs

A Medical Student's Reflections
on Theology and Human Health

Internal Organs

A Medical Student's Reflections
on Theology and Human Health

Poems by

Douglas Wyatt Anderson

© 2024 Douglas Wyatt Anderson. All rights reserved.
This material may not be reproduced in any form, published,
reprinted, recorded, performed, broadcast,
rewritten or redistributed without
the explicit permission of Douglas Wyatt Anderson.
All such actions are strictly prohibited by law.

Cover design by Shay Culligan

ISBN: 978-1-63980-537-2

Kelsay Books
502 South 1040 East, A-119
American Fork, Utah 84003
Kelsaybooks.com

To my mother and father,
who have patiently seen my writing improve
and encouraged me in my pursuit of God through poetry

Acknowledgments

Some of the poems included in this manuscript were offered publication separately prior to the acceptance of this body of works. Thank you to the following publications:

ALUMNI JOURNAL (Alumni Association School of Medicine of
    Loma Linda University): "Cadaver Talk"
Calla Press: "Manzanita," "Ethylene," "Penumbra"
Ekstasis: "Proprioception," "Expiration Date"

I primarily want to acknowledge my sister, for her original art. Additionally, I'd like to thank my friends Cole Dennis, Andrei Tong, and David Seung for their feedback along the way.

I'd like to also acknowledge Dr. John Walford and Joshua Maxwell for their photographic contributions.

This body of works, Internal Organs, is born of the hours spent in the hospital and classroom. They have served as a way to integrate my faith into what I am learning about medicine and reflect on life as a Christian. I hope that the poems offer praise to God and call others to worship as well.

Contents

I. First Steps

Cadaver Talk	17
Proprioception	19
Furrowed Brow	21
Manzanita	23
Cause of Death	24

II. Growth and Decay

Penumbra	27
Ethylene	29
Expiration Date	31
Battery Acid	33
10:11	35
Usufruct	37

III. Clinical

Pregnant	41
Iron and Iodine	43
Amaurosis fugax	45
Snowpack	47
Detox	49
The Young Man and the Clinic	51
Lifestyle Medicine?	53

IV. You and Me

Oklahoma 1932	57
Worn	59
In the Heat of the Day	61
Interruption and Encounter	63

Tooth and Nail\\Maundy	65
Anchors	67
Parasitic Relationships	68
Bottleneck; Wenckebach	71

V. Day by Day

Dandelions	75
Westward Bound	77
Tangential	79
Clogged	81
Keeping Time	83
Cast Out	84
Night Walk	87
4/23/22	89

. . . begin now to study the little things in your own door yard, going from the known to the nearest related unknown, for indeed each new truth brings one nearer to God.
—George Washington Carver

I. First Steps

These poems were my first attempts at this project, and primarily are concerned with names, parts and wholes, growing old, and reminders. I particularly drew inspiration from the cadaver lab, from the neurology and psychology didactics, and from hikes in the San Jacinto area.

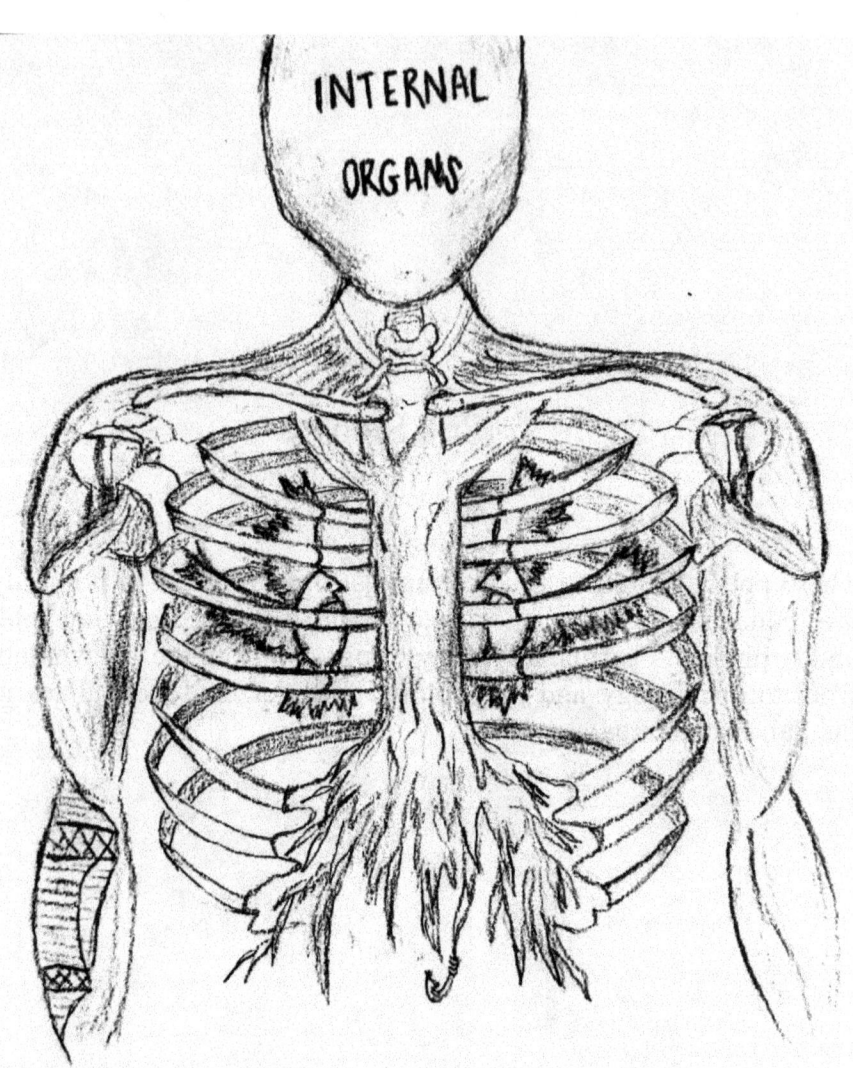

Cadaver Talk

Son of man, can these dry bones live?

O dry bones, when do you become whole
When do your disjointed joints walk alongside another,
When do your sinews embrace,
When does your flesh hold shame and glory?
Tell me exactly when four limbs become
a recipient of divine intervention

As cedar beams slowly weave a temple
You bear more weight than your pieces

All your channels, ports, messengers, pathways, codes
and materials
Can be mapped
Your dust
charted by periods

Until we learn to see breath
We know you not

Proprioception

What do you call this?
For I have forgotten its name
Come to think of it, I forget mine often as well
Placards of what's what
fall right away like Romberg's patients

My walk is unsteady
because nobody told my feet where they are
somewhere along the way I must have lost myelination
on Ariadne's thread
Because how do you call me?
Son? You must be kidding
Beloved? I know we are friends, but . . .
Ransomed? At what cost?
You, who brought order out of nothing,
please remind me where I am

Furrowed Brow

Christ you are the living water
You rush through the world:
Sweeping away the decay, bringing life
You exceed banks, flooding dry plains
Where there was once drought, you bring abundance
You cut through granite stream-beds,
Where there once were hard hearts, they now lie open
You tumble high cliffs,
Where there once was division, there is now unity

My mind is a circuit
Tracks of thought running from one neuron to the next
Canyons and ravines cull and confine my patterned mind
250 miles-an-hour torrents of electricity careening around my skull

Will you not course through my mind?
Will you cut new stream beds in my furrowed brow?
Can I be made a floodplain?
Will you prepare my mind for the harvest?

Lord of untamed waters, come

Manzanita

Right down the middle
Crimson and stone
xylem and phloem
or just old bones

Connections lost, just a frame
flowering, fruiting, all the same

How does it know
what parts must go

Executive functions,
Random draw,
Divine leading:
Hearing your call?

Graceful decline
prolonged yearly
new growth, new fruit
clinging dearly
to the earth
from which it rose
that it may lay down
at last, in graceful repose

Cause of Death

It stared back, that large oblong pupil
of fixed, hardened blood in the pons
Obscuring our view of the former structures
We didn't know what it was
They probably didn't either.
Just a strange artifact of fixation?
No, it was the cause of death,
And what can cause a pontine hemorrhage?
The pathologist shared and asked
A gravestone in a foreign land
suddenly a smoking gun before us
A hidden monument to the dead,
excarnate person we'd been studying for an hour
every gyrus and sulcus laid bare
Something so small to us
Contained a death, grief, loss

II. Growth and Decay

Much of my time in school was spent thinking about my own personal growth through and despite the rigors of academics and life. Each poem contains unique themes, but as a whole they are a testament to grace and an exhortation to trust.

Penumbra

I sit among the fallen Johnny Macs
Their saccharine decay bringing droves of heavy, drunken bees
To the now soft and wrinkled fruits
The dusty tree's shade is complete, and in the penumbra I rest
Caught between sleep and wake
It will all come back one day, every bruised and rotting fruit
reperfused.
In the late summer sun, the shadows grow long
But don't you know?
They will recede again

Ethylene

Plumes of ethylene settle around my fast-ripening oranges
"What is it?"
They seem to say
"This isn't the sixth day.
Don't let us remain until morning"
Chemically coordinated abundance

Wild oak trees keep this tucked away in their whorled brow
and somehow know to wait,
until together they carpet the ground with their starchy progeny;
a mast year

Cicadas too, will hatch in a deafening roar every 17 years
They must keep time in the shallow layers of topsoil,
counting the frost and thaw

Daily bread comes in waves,
if you learn to read the seasons

My eighth-grade biology teacher knew this.
He would individually hide his bananas around the house
in an attempt to dis-coordinate their breathy maturation

Mid-western congregants grace unlocked sedans and minivans
with goliath zucchinis

Look, a table is prepared for you
If you hold it yourself, it will truly rot away

Expiration Date

Each day, You call me to die
And I imagine a slow fade, with some final, quiet exhalation
in some distant room
but maybe also
I need to die differently
Each day
like my ballpoint pen
with inky abundance in death
The last light of the western sun illuminating radiant falling leaves
Or a child on the verge of a meltdown
running around the room
Or a Bilbo Baggins eleventy-oneth birthday
Trusting that all that is left behind
is so much less than what lies ahead

Battery Acid

I like trying to grow things
putting seeds in the ground
watering and trusting.
Then one day, when all hope that the seeds were viable was lost,
little green shoots and cotyledons

I sometimes forget to water them.
Often the plants don't survive

Checking old remotes never fails to surprise me.
What? These batteries crusted over already?

Turn away for but a moment
And acid corrodes your inattention.

But sometimes my plants make it, on their own,
just there waiting for the rain

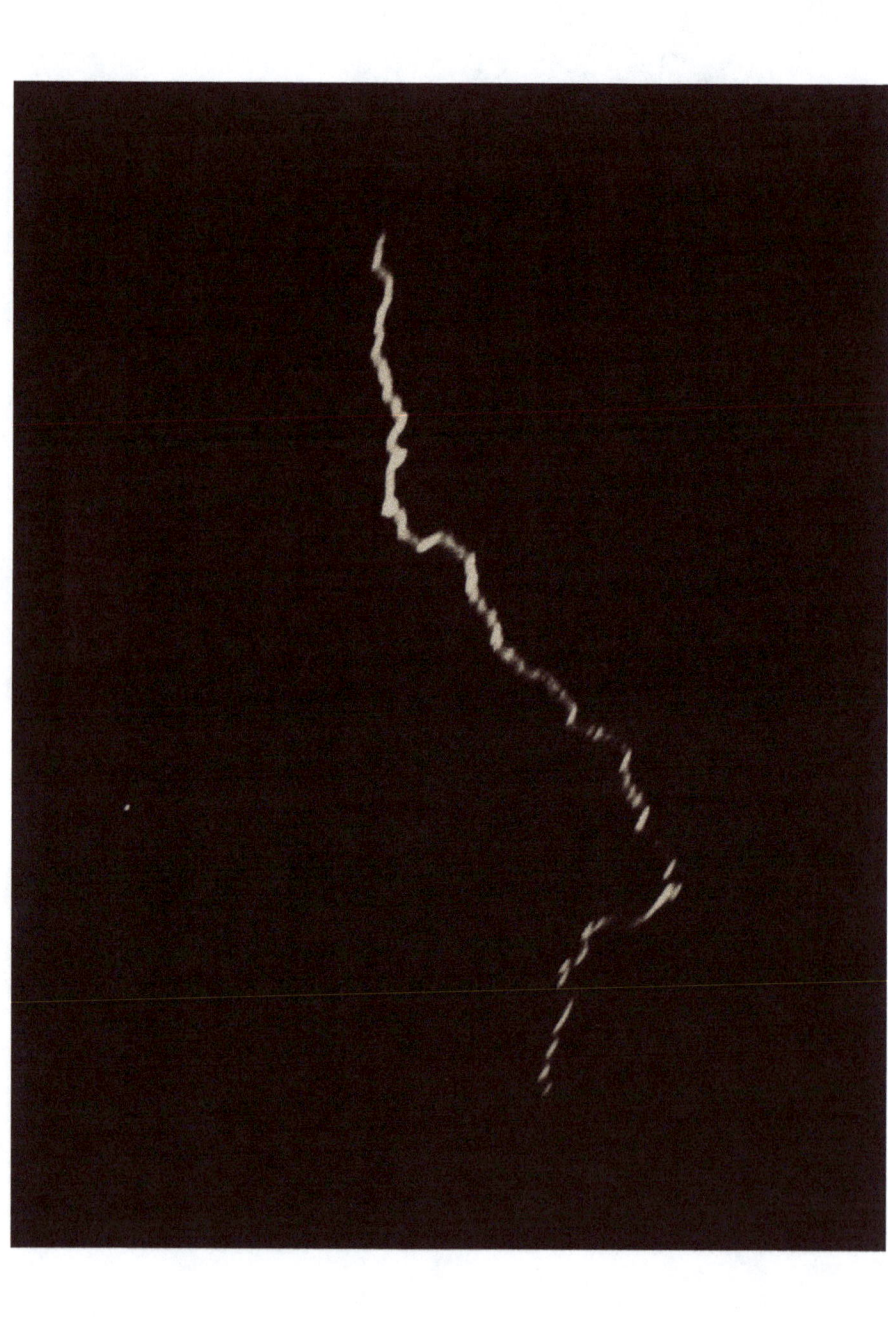

10:11

Did you notice?
The cottonwood slowly waned yellow and brown
in some forgotten valley behind the palm and evergreen.
Hawthorne bramble bare were the hills,
when I got around to looking
It comes on suddenly,
Late night LED-led sessions on the courts cut short at 10:11
New hospital hallways with withdrawal fasciculations,
photophobia, dialysis absentees, and diabetic neuropathies
Lukewarm coffee on old gutted expresso machines and split pine
Not many leaves fall here
Just a slight smell of decay
Will you preserve the good,
When all seems to die away?

Usufruct

*Man has too long forgotten that the earth was given to him for usufruct alone,
not for consumption, still less for profligate waste.*
—Marsh, Man and Nature

Dig up your buried talents
Till your kiln fired hearts
For are you not too earth?

Rows and rows pass by
Knee high corn pulsing out the window of your sedan
Leggy insects pop and splatter
year after year of mono-cropping and shallow roots

Dark room woven images of falling protons
respond to fields
showing more of the same
surfacing white and grey out of some black lake

Planting what
metallic clink of shovel and silver
It neither gives nor takes
it is dead

There is no call for
pegged Long John Silvers,
but for patient waiting
shelterbelts, pruning, and terracing
Cycles of light and rain.

III. Clinical

This collection serves as a reflection on my experiences in and around the hospital. These do not represent individual interactions I have had, but synthesize realizations about human nature and station.

Pregnant

Inflatable leaves rise and fall,
as the wind animates and fills their delicate membranes
drawn in, pushed out
untapped dark pools lie, profound,
amidst the cedar and pomegranate
mycorrhizae established, delicately knit together in utero
endometrium, hyphae, breath, stomata, pillars, bones
I lose track, you reside within, but are the vine
Sustaining all, yet once sustained by fleshy stem and roots
What are you bearing up?

Iron and Iodine

It turns to bronze, elemental sanitation
framed in blue sheets
earthy, sweet, and mellow
a deft, straight line
then harsh wisps of smoke rise
followed by the metallic smell of multitudinous messengers

You were there, but far away
buried in blue
should I think of your eyes
at a time like this?

Your avascular planes start to separate
How hard it is to remember you early in the morning,
Shaking the sleep from your speech.
So quickly it all becomes Iron and Iodine, Carbon and Sulfur
Can my eyes bring both into focus?
It's a thin veil,
but thousands of years stand between

SHAKSPEARE.
King Lear

Amaurosis fugax

All it takes is one unexpected notification
a couple of words, previously unsaid
some distant machination of nations
a slip of a surgeon's hand
one more nanometer of cloggage in already narrowed lumens
How can they tear your sternum in two,
but one microscopic pebble will render you speechless?
For the rest of your life
Sudden darkness
Will you stay with me in my ruddy fragility
in times of curtains falling down

Snowpack

Not just San Jacinto, San Gorgonio, and Baldy,
Down to spine, scale, and scorch.
Snowfall in southern California

It's a classic, the clock quivering with excitement
At the side of my bed; bells and hammer poised.
It is so ready to wake me.
Poor thing, I've been up for hours

I breathe in the unfamiliar air whose scent I can no longer smell,
Hit the clock at 6am,
And throw on my jeans and t-shirt.
These still smell like home.

Like stale smoke, like loud voices, like my siblings.
I join my new siblings around the table
(not crowded with crushed beer cans)
She pours the milk on our many bowls

I'm a liability, and they know it
At least she does
Don't worry, I won't be here long
I never am

But she smiles warmly, and tells me to wear a jacket today.

And yet snow falls on southern California
Despite all the predictions and generations without
Despite CPS raids and substance abuse. They are your inheritance
Experts wonder, could it be enough?

Detox

Every step bloomed detritus
The clear water obscured by
broken down leaves, needles, and runoff dirt

In my arms, one of Wisconsin's finest melons
coated thoroughly with bacon grease from this morning's breakfast
Other campers scrambling behind me though the waist deep water
fish watching from under the dock

Remember how it felt, that slippery weight,
the oncoming onslaught of kids
That brief moment where you see it all getting away from you

I don't trust myself to hold much these days
waking up to monitor my vitals
tapered medications to control the shaking in my hands

There was this log, stripped of bark,
anchored on either cut end, but freely rotating
it feels a little like that first step where you know it's a wash
coming up for air soon enough to see it all falling away

The Young Man and the Clinic

The old man shuffles into your clinic;
his hands raw and his feet unshod
I stand there in my Bermuda shirt and flip-flops
He asks about DeMaggio this year
"My left hand has seized up recently," he tells me.
"A warm compress and stretches will help"
I give antibiotics for his hands and rope-burn on his back
A dermatology referral for the sunspots

"Is that a shark's carcass?"
He smiles painfully a moment, and then shakes his head no

Lifestyle Medicine?

Lord, somewhere along the 15-min blocks of time
I charted you in
Right between 30-min of cardio
And a meal filled with whole grains

Depression prophylaxis, I think would be the unofficial name
I gave this time
Somewhere I forgot that you are not an SSRI
But my God, who promises not the easy, gentle road

But a life of searching and of finding

A promise of company in times of despair
Not necessarily the correct cocktail of molecules
To take the edge off

A promise that you are renewing and redeeming,
Even when I do not see it or feel it.

A promise that you, my God,
Are worth every tear, every restless night, every slow exhale

IV. You and Me

Thoughts on knowing people, knowing God, and the difficulties and beauty therein.

GESCHÄFTS-BÜCHER-SCHNITTE.
Englisch Marmor.
1farbig mit Untergrund.

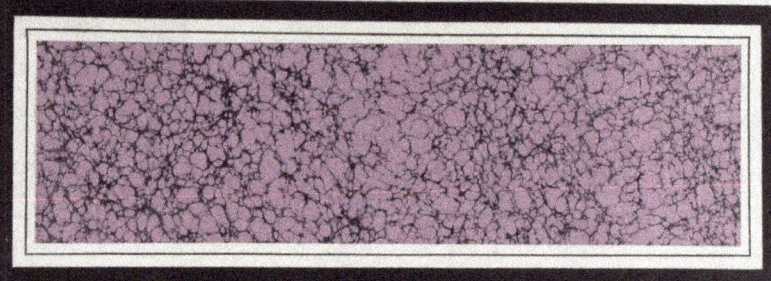

Oklahoma 1932

Don't bother wiping them
Window sills crusted with
Saw teeth biting
and oxen unzipping the earth
and year after year of thin margins; planted again

Light finds its way through
Illuminating you and me,
upside-down plates and upside-down cups

I try to set still, each movement
teaches flight to our fallen skin and the exiled topsoil, intermingled

The boundaries between you and me
thin as the floor storehouses our dust

your ears, a quivering drum
the back of your eyes, a shingled layer 2–3 deep
your nose, rootlets burrowing through bone
deep in your chest, it's just one layer thick;
a narrow border

Despite all this,
I still cannot see your face as it is

but if you'll sit with me
maybe our lungs will filter and still the suspending air

Old Trapper.

Notman, Photo.

Worn

A gentle wave of tar and stone falls softly behind
staunchly pressed, until smooth, dark and ongoing
grooved rubber glides over quietly until eventually,
the rubber is bald and the individual stones
gather and drift against the lapping of vehicles

Shhk! Shhk! Shhk!
rhythmically plunged into the earth: metal and wood
the blade notched, scraped, and rusting
the handle thinning where held
lifting dust, dirt, sand, clay

Friction and time are the same

but never have you met an old person
ever new is the person next to you
abraded and exfoliated by the sand of the hourglass
their keratinocytes overturned

In the Heat of the Day

Each year before the heat of summer,
the Chinese elms are trimmed to their bones
to what end I don't know, as our once shady street
now creates tiny green houses in all the street parked cars
Amber rain weeps from the scarring scabs
as waxy new leaves reclaim a fraction of their former fullness

I imagine if left fully clad in delicate leaves,
what subterranean water is left would be siphoned by the heat
through the many thin green outlets.
Much better are the thick, scaly limbs left floating in the sun.
At least, that's what I tell myself

I still want to speak your name, my friend
weeping amber rain
We stood side by side, branches knitting a complete shade
but spears of sun found their way through

Interruption and Encounter

Wordless request, reflexive denial at the ARCO
Oh, wait, yes please
Reused window cleaner and pulpy paper towels
What is your name?
Two fingers held up, Peace? Two?
No, not that, ok
Click
Looks great!
Signals just a moment, and cleans even the side mirrors
Sorry I don't sign
I don't have paper and pen
I do have a phone
Victor!
Nice to have met you Victor, thanks for the wash.
Are you here often?
I come here every two weeks.

Washed again, when I least expected it
Lord, you speak through the mute.

Tooth and Nail\\Maundy

Why do I reverberate?
Bristling with frequencies I receive
Till all this place knows the tune

I step out,
Hoping the desert will absorb, deaden
Let me be a resistor
The field is empty, grass mostly sun-dried now
Let me be a cover of snow
A red-tailed hawk dangles above
Let me be oil on the surface
Geckos flee before me
And if I cannot,
Grant me still the grace to repent

In the desert, water sprinkles sidewalks and lawns at certain hours
Today, by some fault, the sidewalk became a pool,
A basin in the desert,
Before I noticed,
My feet were submerged; washed

Praise be to the God of rivers in the desert,
Who still washes feet

Anchors

Be thou my vision
Oh unimaged Father
My heart sometimes needs a cue
Something to place in my network of knowing
some visual stimuli to tie to your name.
My ears long to turn my head to a place
What is your voice like?
Will I recognize it?
For all my hours of pursuit,
how many misperceptions still
need to be burned away?
In the shadow of Mount Gerizim
I worship what I don't know

Parasitic Relationships

He who was seated on the throne said, "I am making everything new!"
Then he said, "Write this down, for these words are trustworthy and true."
—Revelation 21:5

Husbands and Wives. Mothers and Daughters. Fathers and Sons.
Sisters and Brothers.
Ones and Zeros, Satellite Signals, Crests and Troughs, Dots and
Dashes, Paper and Ink blotted
Human Contact

B   R   O   K   E   N

The world awaits, through baited breath, waiting as the prey
become the bouncer, and as all our conversations end in Babel.

Maybe one day we will sing together
Bring each other
Closer to another
But for now no cover
From the lack luster
Relations of stolen Father Mother Sister Brother

Creation Groans
Bare branches creak, streams weep,
Fires rage and mountains tumble

We said let me taste, then we ran, then we ceased. No longer can
we be with one who made us

Our lives' cycles became so frightful
We turned our eyes to other food sources
Group forces cause displacement within,
and we end up in sin

Fiery serpents, kissing bugs, relentless cough, where are the drugs
that break these cycles
That so enticed us

Twisted and abused,
Used for the purposes of satan's coups
They wait alongside us

For all creation groans
Waiting for his throne
To come again and right us

Bottleneck; Wenckebach

One-way valves; integral
that compartmentalize
atria | ventricle
For better or for worse

Score countless tracts alike
they here all must converge
the AV node; the dike
for richer or poorer

rings insulate advance
clock weights rest unwound here
Can conductance enhance?
In sickness and in health

It sure feels like flutter

V. Day by Day

As I grow older, it seems that less and less are the days when my perspective on life changes radically. That said, the way I view the world is constantly being tweaked. These are some of those small realizations.

Dandelions

They are always floating by
Little seeds of worry
Waiting for fertile soil
little poofs on the wind
wipe them from your mind
or wait them out
floater in your eye

But sometimes they take
and the more you scratch,
they find cracks in
flourishing little castaways
some pustule
that calls for attention in the mirror
transformed from a puff
to a weight unbearable

let me laugh until it is
once again just a breath
and the land is clear
for my apple and pear saplings

Westward Bound

Captures the imagination,
Don't it?
Be it the piebald, barn owl, paint splatter skies
Or just the unclaimed acres;
Foretaste of potential, aftertaste of dirt
Last stake strikes are long gone
Canned in cellars of American psyche

If we're not going west, we're going home
How did we get way out here?
Never thought I'd drown in so much sky
What I'd give for the silence of an old friend

Don't make fun
We're all going somewhere
Trailheads beckon, glassy seas call
Wistful glances at the birds
Aristophanes slyly nods

Tangential

Keep your eyes on me
You say
How this has anything to do
With the water about my feet
I do not know

Alkali metal lithium
Swallowed daily stops
profligate spending, insomnia, and grandiosity
But how?
This we don't yet know

I must not understand
the pathophysiology of being human
because when I tell you
my relationships lie broken
my mind wrestles with my stomach
my knee echoes these aches
your response is the same:
keep your eyes on me,
we will address them along the way

Clogged

She steps into ankle-high water
cursing her own follicular turnover
cold feet, warm shoulders

The Keurig stops halfway through inhalation,
blinking descale

her Corolla starts tentatively, and dies as the throttle peddles down
the mechanic asks about recent replacement of the air intake filter

Where are the dratted mesangial cells of shower drains?

Keeping Time

His hand glides across the antiquated chalkboard
loved dearly still by mathematicians and chemists
a quiet flurry of white dust falling from the excoriated tip.
The lines are smooth, confident, and quickly drawn.
His hand moves away, and again, his head starts to bob,
as if affirming the structures he still can create
His arm trembles as he explains
the syntax and tempo of the shifting bonds.
The metronome keeps pace, but its arc grows wider and wider
eventually the familiar molecules wouldn't contain its ticking
"The chemicals don't bother me anymore," he said
"All laboratory chemists lose their smell eventually"
I still see him sometimes shuffling around the indoor track
—head and arms keeping time
I think to myself, someone give this man a piece of chalk

Cast Out

"You soiled the bed, again"
"I have?"
"Yes, just like you." The nurse smiles, not meaning to chide
The wrinkled face wrinkles a little more
Remembering nothing else
I am incontinent
"Let's get you cleaned up; you have a visitor"

Walking along sun-dried hills after work
Heard it first
And then saw it, bristling with potential hurt
Coiled, mouth agape, head cocked back slightly

He looks the same, somehow
"Hi dad," starts an ancient young man
"Uh-huh," responds the elder, cautiously, not meeting his eyes
That's all it took
"You won't even look at me dad? Just like the day you kicked me out. I needed you that day, and you never even looked me in the eye"
"Uh-huh"
Louder now. "I can see why mom divorced you and left you here to die"
Old eyes turn to meet sunken younger eyes
Abruptly the later turn and walk away

That's who I was?

Shouting wafts in from the hall
Then a women drags the sunken eyes back in by the sweatshirt
"Tell him you're sorry,"
Demands the women, the other looking decidedly limp
"Didn't know you were coming"

She turns brilliant red
"Is this what you do? Come in day after day without us and poison him?"
His sunken eyes do not meet hers
"Dad, you kicked him out of the house twenty years ago, but it was because his was stealing Mom's jewelry for meth. You cried that day"
Turning in the direction of her brother. "He cried that day"
"And what's more, Mom didn't divorce you. She died. I'm sorry."

An old man cries in his recliner in a nursing home, a daughter puts her hand on his shoulder, and a son stands caught in a corner.

"Don't let him in anymore"

Night Walk

Do they wake you?
These high mounted nightlights
filtering sweetly through the weeping pepper trees
They look fossilized in sepia hues of green
others look on, bundles of lines and turpentine-scented stars

A water-tower perched on spindly legs leaps out of some
bygone age, and soft thunder shakes the ground
As long mechanical beasts run their courses in the night.
What is one more weight to them, on their broad backs?
To me, a portal to a new world by the time morning is born

A churn of hisses and rushing air
Shhh, I tell my heart
Slow your frenzied pace,
it's not that
but it does not so quickly forget.
Then, underground rain falling up and down again

Across the street, a silent watcher on the lamppost
Surveying the waste,
Hidden in the halo
a muffled whoosh

4/23/22

Every Manzanita, a burning bush
Every cedar, a pillar of your temple
Every pine needle triad, a rosary
Every Coulter and Sugar pine, a living censer
Every step, a pilgrimage
Every oak, with light filtering through, a stained glass.
Shall I leave my shoes on, my Lord?
Every step I take is on holy ground.
Will you wash my feet in snow and runoff

Bibliography

Cadaver Talk:
- Bella Oliver
  Metaphorical Anatomy, 2023
  Pencil and paper

Proprioception:
- Joshua Maxwell
  Every Day Maze, 2023
  Digital

Furrowed Brow:
- Frank Meadow Sutcliffe (British, 1853–1941), photographer
  [Flooded street], 1890–1900
  Gelatin silver print
  Image: 18.1 × 28.4 cm (7 1/8 × 11 3/16 in.), Mount: 19.9 × 30 cm (7 13/16 × 11 13/16 in.)
  The J. Paul Getty Museum, Los Angeles, 84.XM.496.10
  www.getty.edu/art/collection/object/1045YS

Manzanita:
- Douglas Wyatt Anderson
  Manzanita Bush, September 2021
  Digital

Penumbra:
- John Walford
  Frail Frames in Spring Time, April 16th 2004
  Digital
  www.flickr.com/photos/walford/2419045342/in/album-72157614586483376/

Ethylene:
- Pieter Bruegel the Elder (Netherlandish, Breda (?) ca. 1525–1569 Brussels)
  The Harvesters, 1565
  Oil on Wood
  Image: Overall, including added strips at top, bottom, and right, 46 7/8 x 63 3/4 in. (119 x 162 cm); original painted surface 45 7/8 x 62 7/8 in. (116.5 x 159.5 cm)
  The Metropolitan Museum of Art, New York City, 19.164
  www.metmuseum.org/art/collection/search/435809

Expiration Date:
- Douglas Wyatt Anderson
Lone Maple, October 2016
Digital

Battery Acid:
- Douglas Wyatt Anderson
Southern Illinois isn't so bad, January 2019
Digital

10:11:
- Charles Moussette (French, active 1880s)
[Spiral of Lightning in a Thunderstorm], May 12, 1886
Albumen silver print from glass negative
Mount: 9 13/16 in. × 6 7/8 in. (25 × 17.5 cm)
Image: 6 5/8 × 4 5/8 in. (16.9 × 11.7 cm)
The Metropolitan Museum of Art, New York City, 2005.100.651
www.metmuseum.org/art/collection/search/287289

Usufruct:
- Rothstein, Arthur, (1915-1985)
Dust bowl farmer raising fence to keep it from being buried under drifting sand. Cimarron County, Oklahoma, 1936 Apr.
1 negative: nitrate
Image: 2 1/4 x 2 1/4 inches or smaller.
Library of Congress Prints and Photographs Division Washington, D.C., LC-USF34- 004051-E [P&P] LOT 521
www.loc.gov/pictures/item/2017760334/

Pregnant:
- George Hitchcock (America, 1850-1913)
The Annunciation, 1887
Oil on canvas
Image: 158.8 × 204.5 cm (62 1/2 × 80 1/2 in.)
The Art Institute of Chicago, Chicago, Potter Palmer Collection, 1930.1289
www.artic.edu/artworks/7503/the-annunciation

Iron and Iodine:
- Unknown (Greek (Attic))
Attic Female Head Vase Fragment, 5th century B.C.
Terracotta Object: 4.9 cm (1 15/16 in.)
The J. Paul Getty Museum, Villa Collection, Malibu, California, Gift of Gordon McLendon, 76.AE.102.23
www.getty.edu/art/collection/object/103T7D

Amaurosis Fugax:
- Engraver: Richard Earlom (British, London 1743–1822 London); Artist: After Henry Fuseli (Swiss, Zürich 1741–1825 London)
King Lear Casting Out His Daughter Cordelia (Shakespeare, King Lear, Act 1, Scene 1), first published 1792; reissued 1852.
Stipple engraving; fourth state of four. Image: 17 3/8 x 23 11/16 in. (44.1 x 60.1 cm), plate: 19 1/2 x 25 1/8 in. (49.5 x 63.8 cm), sheet: 21 3/4 x 27 15/16 in. (55.3 x 71 cm).
The Metropolitan Museum of Art, Gertrude and Thomas Jefferson Mumford Collection, Gift of Dorothy Quick Mayer, 1942, 42.119.540
www.metmuseum.org/art/collection/search/354230

Snowpack:
- Douglas Wyatt Anderson
Green Field with Snowy Peak
Digital

Detox:
- Unknown Woodsman
Moments Before, October 2016
Digital

The Young Man and the Clinic:
- Allen & Ginter (American, Richmond, Virginia)
English Tourist, from World's Dudes series (N31) for Allen & Ginter Cigarettes, 1888
Commercial color lithograph
Sheet: 2 3/4 x 1 1/2 in. (7 x 3.8 cm)
The Metropolitan Museum of Art, New York City, 63.350.202.31.46
www.metmuseum.org/art/collection/search/411311

Lifestyle Medicine?:
- Douglas Wyatt Anderon
Flight Amidst Structure, January 2024
Digital

Oklahoma 1932:
- Unknown Artist
  Musterbuch von Marmor Schnitten für Geschäfts-Bücher, 1870
  Material not documented
  Height: 12 5/8 × 15 3/4 in. (32 cm)
  The Metropolitan Museum of Art, New York City, Z271.3.M37 M87 1870 Quarto
  www.metmuseum.org/art/collection/search/892137

Worn:
- William Notman (Canadian, born Scotland, 1826–1891)
  Old Trapper, 1867
  Albumen silver print
  Image: 13 × 8.5 cm (5 1/8 × 3 3/8 in.)
  Mount: 19.7 × 12.7 cm (7 3/4 × 5 in.)
  The J. Paul Getty Museum, Los Angeles, 84.XB.935.21.1
  www.getty.edu/art/collection/object/108W59

In the Heat of the Day
- Douglas Wyatt Anderson
  Peruvian Pink Pepper Tree Under Street Lamp, August 2021
  Digital

Tooth and Nail\\Maundy:
- MODIS Rapid Response Team
  Snow in the Atacama Desert, November 2011
  Digital
  NASA Earth Observatory, unknown reference number
  earthobservatory.nasa.gov/images/151533/on-this-day-in-2011-snow-in-the-atacama-desert

Anchors:
- Douglas Wyatt Anderson
  Galicia Sunrise, June 2017
  Digital

Parasitic Relationships:
- Unknown (Greek (Attic))
  Fragment of an Attic Black-Figure Stemless Kylix, late 6th–early 5th century B.C.
  Terracotta Object (greatest extent): 4.5 × 7.4 cm (1 3/4 × 2 15/16 in.)
  The J. Paul Getty Museum, Villa Collection, Malibu, California, 81.AE.206.D.1526

Bottleneck; Wenckebach:
- Douglas Wyatt Anderson
  Evening Rose, May 2023
  Digital

Dandelions:
- Barbara Regina Dietzsch (German, 1706–1783)
  Dandelion, about 1755
  Watercolor and gouache, on vellum, bordered in gold
  Unframed: 29 × 21 cm (11 7/16 × 8 1/4 in.)
  The J. Paul Getty Museum, Los Angeles, 2004.147
  www.getty.edu/art/collection/object/1097QJ

Keeping Time:
- Douglas Wyatt Anderson
  Pop-pop in Stereo Set Reflection, August 20218
  Digital

Night Walk:
- Douglas Wyatt Anderson
  Evening in the Upper Peninsula, October 2016
  Digital

Westward Bound:
- Douglas Wyatt Anderson
  Not a Bad Place to Make a Living, June 2018
  Digital

Tangential:
- Douglas Wyatt Anderson
  Which Way Up?, June 2017
  Digital

4/23/22:
- Douglas Wyatt Anderson
  Morning on San Jacinto, October 2021
  Digital

About the Author

Douglas "Wyatt" Anderson is a poet and medical student. He spends most of his days trying to learn all that is necessary to care well for his future patients. However, he also writes. He writes to integrate the various interests (theology, botany, and medicine), to reflect on the world around him, and ultimately to praise God.